Falling Brick Kills Local Man

THE FELIX POLLAK PRIZE IN POETRY

Falling Brick Kills Local Man

Mark Kraushaar

THE UNIVERSITY OF WISCONSIN PRESS

The University of Wisconsin Press
1930 Monroe Street, 3rd Floor
Madison, Wisconsin 53711-2059

www.wisc.edu/wisconsinpress/

3 Henrietta Street
London WC2E 8LU, England

Copyright © 2009
The Board of Regents of the University of Wisconsin System
 All rights reserved. No part of this publication may be reproduced, stored in a retrieval system, or transmitted, in any format or by any means, digital, electronic, mechanical, photocopying, recording, or otherwise, or conveyed via the Internet or a Web site without written permission of the University of Wisconsin Press, except in the case of brief quotations embedded in critical articles and reviews.

5 4 3 2 1

Printed in the United States of America

Library of Congress Cataloging-in-Publication Data
Kraushaar, Mark.
 Falling brick kills local man / Mark Kraushaar.
   p. cm. — (The Felix Pollak prize in poetry)
 Poems.
 ISBN 978-0-299-23080-7 (hardcover : alk. paper) —
 ISBN 978-0-299-23084-5 (pbk. : alk. paper) —
 ISBN 978-0-299-23083-8 (e-book)
 I. Title. II. Series: Felix Pollak prize in poetry (Series)
PS3561.R295F35   2009
811'.54—dc22   2008038483

Book design: David Alcorn, Alcorn Publication Design

For Stephanie
And in memory of
Chris St. George and Nils Watson

For here, the moment all the spaces along the road between here and there—which the young know are infinite and all others know are not—get used up, that's it.

—Galway Kinnell, "The Road Between Here and There"

Contents

How Lives Move Forward in the
  Same Moments *3*
Stupid *5*
Everything *7*
We Regret to Inform *8*
I Want the Power to Go Out *10*
At the Greyhound Station *11*
At Sherman and First *13*
American Golden Eagle Flyer *14*
Express *17*
US Exhaust and Tire *19*
Gum *21*
In Line at the Kwik Trip *23*
Heat *25*
Water Squirrels *27*
Dick and Jane *29*
I Controlled Paul Molitor's Hitting Streak *31*
Dear Mr. Whitman *33*
Ray *35*
Les Waverly: Secrets in Conversation *36*
Fast Loans *38*
Personal Reasons *40*
Twenty-something *42*
We Choose Our Parents *43*
The Call *45*
Wichita 67204 *47*
An Old Story *49*
Valley Road *51*
Edward Hopper, Morning Sun 1952 *52*

Chloral Hydrate 500mg May Repeat Times One
   as Needed for Sleeplessness   *54*
1-900-CHAT   *56*
WWII Plane Found on Moon   *58*
Ming's Imperial Palace, October 1975   *60*
Free Throw   *62*
House of Chong   *64*
Kodachrome   *65*
Road Kill   *66*
Bat Boy Escapes   *67*
Falling Brick Kills Local Man   *68*
Jack   *70*
Schuster   *72*
Unencumbered   *74*
The Message   *76*
Tonight   *77*
Prognostic   *79*
This Is What Happened   *80*
Mantra   *82*

Acknowledgments

Acknowledgement is made to the following publications in which some of the poems in this book first appeared, sometimes in slightly different versions:

Another Chicago Magazine: "Batboy Escapes"
The Beloit Poetry Journal: "Jack," "Dear Mr. Whitman"
Cincinnati Review: 1-900-CHAT
The Crab Orchard Review: "Stupid"
The Gettysburg Review: "I Want the Power to Go Out," "We Regret to Inform," "Everything," "This Is What Happened," "Tonight," "Falling Brick Kills Local Man"
Kansas Quarterly: "American Golden Eagle Flyer"
Margie: "Dick and Jane"
Montserrat Review: "US Exhaust and Tire"
Poetry East: "Ray," "At Sherman and First," "Twenty-something"
Poetry Northwest: "Express," "At the Greyhound Station," "House of Chong," "Wichita 67204," "WWII Plane Found on Moon," "Fast Loans," "I Controlled Paul Molitor's Hitting Streak," "Water Squirrels"
Shenandoah: "How Lives Move Forward in the Same Moments," "Free Throw," "Road Kill," "Mantra"
Southern Poetry Review: "We Choose Our Parents"
The Spoon River Poetry Review: "Chloral Hydrate 500mg May Repeat Times One as Needed for Sleeplessness"

Texas Review: "The Message"
Third Coast: "Prognostic"

Some of these poems appeared previously in a chapbook entitled *How Lives Move Forward in the Same Moments* (Flying White Press); "Tonight" also appears in *The Best American Poetry 2006* (Scribner); "Free Throw," in *Motion: American Sports Poems* (University of Iowa Press); "Ray," in *Who Are the Rich and Where Do They Live? Anthology of Poetry from the Pages of Poetry East*; and "Dear Mr. Whitman," in *Visiting Walt: Poems Inspired by the Life and Work of Walt Whitman* (University of Iowa Press).

I am grateful to many who have provided invaluable help with these poems over the years, among them Chuck Cantrell, Richard Merelman, Mark Kliewar, and Richard Rowe.

Special thanks to David Wagoner and Robin Seyfried for their encouragement early on. Thanks also to the University of Wisconsin Press and to Marilyn Nelson for choosing this manuscript.

Falling Brick Kills Local Man

How Lives Move Forward in the Same Moments

In Maine one day
a man winds his watch
while taking a leak. Suddenly,
distracted by a child's shout
or a train passing or the busy,
gray fabric of his life so far,
he pisses on his shoes. He pauses,
looks down, and begins to curse.
Meanwhile, and by this I mean
at the same time precisely,
in Seoul or Arena or Kiev
another man nods yes and then
yes again, it is late
and he'll have to start home after all.
This is at his best friend's house
up the street. It's snowing.
He pulls out his scarf
and stands up. But it's strange
all this, it's odd
how lives move in the same
moments so softly forward. How
a lady selling baked clay beads
in Marrakech, let's say, leans
against a blue stucco wall
and thinks of penmanship or fresh fruit
while a boy in Dubuque starts work
at a five-and-ten-cent store
stamping figurines. It's almost

a dance, I mean, or it's
nearly musical the way some days
one man's speech keeps time
with another man's coughing
or washing or writing reports. It's
uncanny how as some man in Bangor,
Maine, steps out of the bushes
stamping his two flat feet in the leaves
some other man in those same, invisible
wide moments closes his best friend's closet
and, dusting off his hat, starts home.

Stupid

What if,
because of the familiar sound
of a particular voice, a boy's dog comes when called.
Come here girl, Good girl, and, *Good Judy,*
so she trots straight over, tail quickly swishing.
Now what if one late afternoon the boy
arrives home after a day at the park
where he's stabbed a bullet line drive
thus assuring his own star status
and saving the day for the Fritz
Spray Paint Blue Devils.
Or maybe he's struck out four times,
heaving his bat at the backstop, swearing
it's all the fault of the too bright sun
or his too tight and wrong color uniform.
Head down for shame or for speed,
he pedals home, drops his yellow bike, and runs
past the mailbox, over the lawn, as his dad
steps off the front porch
sipping a Pabst.
Now, supposing next, to show
how a dog responds not to the meaning
of words but to their timbre and pitch, the dad
claps twice and calls, crooning in the kindest tone,
Here Dimwit, and *Come Dumbbell.*
Once again the dog bounds straight over
and sits or jumps up or lies on her back, legs
churning away as though speeding
through the blue heavens upside down.

The dad strokes her belly with his whole palm.
But what if, because he would himself feel too stupid
to mention how cruel this seems,
the boy won't find a single right thing
to say, won't try to, won't want to.
Instead, idly improving upon
the pocket of his mitt with his fist,
he stands where he is looking on, stands there,
and, removing his cap, then pauses
a moment, as the sun, three minutes lower,
begins now to make a shadow in the shape of a boy,
aged eleven, by a tree, glove on one hand,
cap in the other.

Everything

You could say it started when she'd
crossed the lawn, so maybe it did.
You could say it started as
she'd lain in the hammock or noticed the clouds.
However it worked it was as if half the too tenanted
past appeared, botched trip, ungiven hello,
Whooz-it, So-and-So and so on.
She closed her eyes.
She opened her eyes
and examined the spilt tea
which beside its quartered lemon
sparkled in the mown grass and watered
the ground which fed the trees that reached
the sky we say is endless and that she,
looking up, felt lifted by, felt a part of—
it was something like that—this lifted,
floating unknowingness.
And that's what happened.
You could say it started when she'd entered
the kitchen or as she'd moved
by her husband or when she'd rinsed
the blue cup and thought
of the moment she lived in.
But you could say it started when
she'd stood at the window, so maybe it did.
Or you could say it started when she'd crossed
the lawn or when she'd turned
and said, said or thought, What then,
referring to everything, *is* this contraption?

We Regret to Inform

> You do it with love, even if you think war
> is stupid.
>> JANICE MANN SEWING NAME TAGS ON UNIFORMS FOR
>> SOLDIERS HEADED TO THE MIDEAST FROM FORT STEWART,
>> GEORGIA, QUOTED IN *NEW YORK TIMES*

Padilla, Spooner, Pratt:
These three I set to walking with their guns
and gear across a bridge and into a town
with snipers whom I render blind.
No harm can come to Reynolds.
Because it's after noon,
because I've laid
white thread beside a hanging ivy,
no harm can come to Overkamp or Silva.
For Switzky bombs are harmless.
And for Rosenthal and Pierce, Namick and Davis,
approaching bullets disappear, and Ingram
and Beam walk with invisible shields.

Long ago, before there was anything,
there was nothing, except that everyone was always
on their way and there would always be
a Jardin and Silverio, always a Greenblatt,
a Fletcher, and a Beinecke,
there would always be a Zachiaris, Uno,
and Jaffe, and never not
a Framstad, a Morris, or a Thayer.
Which is not nothing but something.

If there was nothing first then second
came absence and with absence sadness:
no Fahnstocks, Gaylords, Doerings, or Sidos,
but that would be fixed and finished with.

Often after work I think of them again.
Often at night I think of them as boys
and nameless, climbing off a tractor,
pouring milk, explaining, peeing,
sleeping, snaggle-toothed, pudgy
and whey-faced, brilliant, knock-kneed,
flushed, nervous-laughing, unaccompanied
and acned, handsome and peevish.
No, nothing can touch my Giesen.
No harm can come to Wayfield.
This evening the moon rests
over the trees ironical and sad and still.
I hold my needle in the light for luck.
My Glickstien is charmed,
my Baya blessed.

I Want the Power to Go Out

The way a kid might
she meant making do:
canned supper and candles
and blankets. She meant
the lit sky exploding
water in waves.
She meant lines down.
She meant the power out.
Later she said it
again but more softly.
There was her grandmother
and her mother and myself.
It was raining.
She wore red
and green and black paint on each nail.
She wore blue shoes.
I guessed she
thought of my own week's visit over too soon
as well as let's please not
have an evening with reading
and low voices. I think she meant
the manic lift fear gives as well
as curtains drawn and doors
locked and the lot of us
safe as socks in a drawer.
I guessed she meant the four of us
playing jacks in fact, or spades
or spoons and laughing and talking
louder than ever. I didn't ask.

At the Greyhound Station

This lady'd had her throat
removed. Or it wasn't the whole throat,
no, but the larynx: a laryngectomy.
I guessed she was sixty. Of course,
she couldn't speak or, at least,
not without this little machine
she'd press up under her chin.
But she sat there skinny as a blade
and smoking and looking around when suddenly—
like that—she leaned over and scooped
up this five-year-old.
Well, the boy lit up top to bottom
—completely—
and the two of them sat playing
creature from space because,
of course, that's exactly
what this electric thing sounded like,
an alien—you'd have to hear it.
You speak, I speak, you speak, you
speak, I speak and all
of us waiting for busses were watching this:
myself, the boy's mother, a driver,
and a soldier plus a washroom
attendant by the lockers. But
they sat there, the two of them,
the boy on the lady's lap and
the lady like a talk-show host
back and forth like that until
at the right time the lady tied

the boy's shoe and touched his shirt
and set him down.
Then she walked off toward the counters.
Now, if anyone moved
or looked away for even a moment
I don't know but no one said anything.

At Sherman and First

Or, okay, it was something he'd said,
and regretted, but better he leave.
And so bidden, he did too:
stepped outside
and stood stupid at the curb,
slammed door still sounding.
A little rain fell.
A bicycle slowed
and two girls danced in the yard next door,
but in that seamless
coincidence of place and event
the dancing turned to tag and then a grass fight
and back to dancing
and it seemed so easy—the bright cries
rising, the softening light—
it was as if
by wishing he'd been kinder
he could make it so.

American Golden Eagle Flyer

> Bonus offer. Farmland Set—Only $3
> extra. Includes barn, stotne walls, fences,
> windmill, horses, cows, sheep, chickens,
> pigs, geese, 50 pieces in all!
>   ADVERTISEMENT FROM WEEKLY WORLD NEWS

I've run the stonewall
behind the mill
and on the left, blue
paper for a stream with trout.
Then the tracks
and then the train.
Perfect.
To the far right I've added
a pasture using my own
green towel. Out there
under the best tree I've placed
a couple of horses head to tail.
Of five fences three
wobble and I could probably
send them back
but I've propped sheep
against two and taped the third
until I got them all
just right.
Or more or less.
I've placed the chickens in the pen
and the farmer
by a cow outside the barn.

What I'm saying is the cow
is sick and that the farmer
pays that cow special attention.
I'm saying this farmer
is so worried
he takes tiny white pills
but because I like things mysterious
the cow gets suddenly well.
Later, I walk the farmer
to his truck and tell him,
Go downtown and visit your son,
take a break, see a show together,
have lunch.
As for the geese
I've placed five by the pigs,
two by the house, one on the porch,
and another under.

This works well.
I've placed the rabbits
with the sheep which might not be
precisely right but there's
no more fence and it's good enough.
I've arranged the daughter
and the mother by the stream.
Here I'm saying they're talking
and that the daughter
is terribly angry
and has been with reason for years.
I'm saying that because
it's the most important thing
picture one take the other in her arms.
Notice the daughter's face

and head has a thin, pink ridge
up the nose, over the crown
and down the neck.
You can move it. Careful.
I'm saying, in school
don't they ask the daughter, Hey,
Wendy, too much time on the farm?
Sure they do.
Of course, the ridge
is due to the molding process,
something about it,
technical matters which don't
answer anything.
What I'm saying is that why this happens
and especially why it's happened
to her, no one knows.
But ask around.

Express

On the train of your favorite color,
steam powered and hand fit
and welded for you,
you sit back. For a ride
more suited to you
you couldn't wish.
Out your window
the air is a soft midwestern blue,
and in the distance,
from his field,
a farmer waves.
What isn't your way?
In a few miles,
thinking of you,
thinking only of your happiness,
your conductor stops the train.
Close by you find yourself a shaded spot
and a porter brings your robe
and a chair to match the one at home.
Your feet are bathed,
hair groomed, and soon
because the weather is so nearly perfect
and because you've raised your eyes
in just that way
your lunch is served:
a picnic of seafood and ices
and delicate cakes. Later,
but only when you're ready,

your train rocks gently forward
and you board again.
Even the light across your arm
and hands seems intended for you.
Notice these homes and that bakery,
the cops at the corner,
the girl with the parcel at the five-and-ten.
You see these trees, these elms
with each leaf moving to please you
or console? It's simple.
There is nothing without you.

US Exhaust and Tire

After a long day stacking tailpipe in rows
he arrives home and lies down on the sofa placing
his feet, shoes off, on his hard hat and jacket.
In the distance five identical smokestacks spew
five identical white plumes and if you
were in that room just left of the phone
you'd see that due to the light and cool breeze
each plume turns quickly into an endless
gold streak aimed at the neighboring town.
US Exhaust and Tire—it's where he works.
He turns the TV on.
In a minute, hearing noises behind him,
he starts and sits up to see his daughter
in western pajamas, boots, and blue spurs.
As his wife supports her by the shoulders
the girl sits astride their black Labrador mix.
Dad, she says, Bang, and she waves two red
plastic six guns in every direction, then falls off
sending one gun under the sofa, smashing the other.
Her father jumps up, her mother bends down,
and the little girl begins to laugh and he is,
in this moment, as glad to be where he is
as he has ever been.
The girl crawls after the gun and turns and peeps out
behind the sofa, plugging her father one last time.
He grabs his belly and groans,
slumps forward beside her.
What wouldn't he do?
He'd take a bullet or burn, jump under a train

Name it.
Got me, he says, ugh.
Years later the same man arrives home after a long day
packing staples and pens.
Stemp's Office Supply—he can't complain.
He turns the TV on, walks to the kitchen for a shot
and no more, a little ice.
Possibly tonight he'll open the Pecan Sandies,
finish the Triscuits.
How much has happened though, South Street
divided and widened, his ex-wife moved and remarried.
He naps. And then the landlord calls.
Two cars pass.

Out the window it's a view
like one he remembers: five smokestacks,
identical light, similar plumes aimed eastward to Lincoln.
And how would he not think of his old life,
his pretty daughter, fine, good wife?
And what does he say?
In the same room not five feet away,
you wouldn't hear a thing.

Gum

I've boarded the southbound bus by Walgreen's
when I spot a magazine jammed into the seat
so I pry it out and there's a three-page
spread on heaven
with a full-color photo of Michelangelo's
Last Judgment in which to the left your martyrs
and saints swirl upward past the risen Jesus while
to the right there's a distinctly downward
trend: moneylenders, thieves, and fiends
head straight to the flames.

Is that how it works?
I'm reading along when three young,
largish, and loud-talking women get on at the corner,
and I'm basically minding my
own business when
the one with the lip rings slides in
by an opened window three rows up
and her friend, the biggest and blondest,
parks beside her and, blowing a perfect, purple
bubble, props her knees.

Hey, she says, So I'm out on parole
and I meet this guy, Jimmy, and he's out
on parole so Jimmy goes, Let's party, so like
okay, fine, so pretty soon were like over to my house
and the next morning he's like I thought we was in love,
and I'm like, Whatever, and he's like, As if.

As *if,* I love that,
and I love that post-hipster use of "like"
because it shows, or they both show, how
approximate and multi-meaninged the world
mostly seems, which is exactly what I'm thinking
when with a glance like a slap I'm caught watching
by the third lady, the one in the wobbly heels who teeters
slowly down the aisle and leans over to see what I'm reading
and, placing a hand on my arm and pausing,
straightens and stands there. People,
she says, God, she says, Honestly,
Sweetheart, Mister,
What will be the end?

In Line at the Kwik Trip

The Millionaire was a popular TV show in
the mid-fifties

Whenever that fabulous John Beresford Tipton
summoned his servant Michael Anthony, Presto:
there was smiling Mike in his dark suit
awaiting instructions.
I loved that show.
Mike, he'd say in his raspy, bestowing voice,
Mike, our next millionaire, and then he'd
slowly reach over and hand Mike
that fat check and Mike was off
to find Citizen So-and-So who was always
in a jam with his bookie or his rent or his woman,
and while the money might help
life's big lessons lay with the heart, which
was mostly the theme each week.
But I'm in line at the Kwik Trip
thinking of John Beresford Tipton
when I notice two women hanging a bright
banner of wash behind the parking lot,
little dress, big pants, shirt, shirt,
shirt, and double sheet,
and because their lives can't be easy
or because it's sunny outside, because
it's cool for a change,
because I'm off work for a week
I wish each woman a million
and for a moment the whole scene brightens,

a wheezing diesel pulls up to the sparkling pumps,
the scuttling black cat finds a perch
on the propane cage, but mostly
it's the women I've wished rich,
the first who, arrested in thought, now
stops and crosses her arms
to confer with her friend
who steps sideways past the pants,
past a shirt, and leans forward to listen.

Heat

I'm watching my father
in his naugehyde easy chair
reading the classified.
It's newly warm outside, nearly April,
and he looks up, and he tells me, Get the gloves.
We'll have a catch, he says.
We exit the back door, skirt the soggy lawn,
and take our places in the driveway.
I wing one into the street.
I steam one over his head.
I lean in and heave another, then another and another—
too high, too wide, and too high again and then,
finally, I bonk the wheezing green Dodge
from which my mother emerges,
first frowning a little, then waving once.
I'm throwing heat, I say.
In a week I'll turn thirteen.
In a year I'll start ninth grade.
In ten years I'll have worked as a teacher
and then a waiter and a welder.
In twenty years I'll meet my future ex-wife
at a Citgo in southern Wisconsin.
But what do I know.
And what's my father know
running and lunging for all he's worth?
In thirty years strange tangles and plaques
will enter his brain.
In forty years I'll sit beside him in a featureless,
white condo in Portland, Maine, and when the phone rings,

though he'll pick it up, he'll place it on his head.
Later, twilight turning to dusk,
he'll close his eyes.
The moon will shoot like a thrown blade
through a few clouds skirting an empty tree.
A car door will close, a leaf pile lift softly
off the sidewalk into the breeze.

Water Squirrels

He petted one once and once
a baby ate straight out of his hand.
He swears this is so.
There's four flippers plus a center fin,
weird fur, special gills. He swears to God
this is so and he raises his right hand hope to die,
this twelve-year-old beside the window on the Greyhound
kicking the seat. Or, at least, until the other boy,
the older boy, says,

You're lying.
You're *lying* and there's no such thing.
And here, except for the drone of the motor
and a lady's wet cough, that's it, quiet,
and the younger boy's panic begins,
then sits on his chest like the bully Reason.
But all that's long past and, in fact, right now
it's a sunny afternoon
along the interstate. Cars pass. Birds sing,

and as for the boy with the story he's all grown up
and working for the prison in the town next to his so
imagine him stand on the bed of a pickup.
It's a government truck. He wears a white Stetson
and tall black boots.
He wears a crisp, blue uniform, silver
star, and black wood club. He's a good man,
a good husband and father and this afternoon
he's running a chain gang and carries a shotgun.

He's a good guard.
The men wear orange jumpsuits and small cloth caps
and beyond the road fields turn and a farmer
with his dozen cows heads slowly past a wind-ruined barn.
And what of it?
Well, something, maybe the traffic, maybe a breeze
or the hot sun or the clink clank
of the shovels and picks, something
makes him think of his bus ride thirty years ago,
rocking washroom, greasy seat.

He looks at his men and thinks of this crazy, stupid story,
and he thinks of each man as one more dopey lie
pulling him gently this way, irrevocably that.
Either way pulling his own life
miles out of reach. Why, you know, some days
he'd shoot them then and there, all of them,
without a thought—Pow!
Blam! Blam!—like carnival targets.
And, yes, he would too. But he's a good guard
and a good man and as he raises one hand as if to swear

he's in near perfect accord with what's right and what's real,
in his other hand the dark butt of his twelve gauge
comes to rest on his hip.
He wipes his temple and jaw, takes a long breath as if
to draw all eternity into his lungs as a pebble chip pings
off a hub cap. And in that
moment, 2:14:02 June 6,
whether he blasts away or waves,
his whole life with its lies and near lies and single,
certain truth is once again set in motion as it must be.

Dick and Jane

To think of it now
is to remember there was never
a winter and it never rained. I mean,
there was never a winter and it seemed
the sky was blue and the grass was green.
I mean, I never said, but after school
I'd lie down on my bed and think,
Look Dick,
look up and see.
And when I opened my eyes
I'd see our backyard tree begin to reason,
nodding, wave, and whisper.
Except I liked to play
I was like a little man. I swept and mowed,
I set the table every day, and every
day was filled with fun.
Sally and Jane had fun.
Spot and Puff had fun too.

Over the corner store the poached sun sits.
I can't say, but to think of it now is to wonder
what we should have known.
It's morning.
Galaxies turn, eternities stretch.
As though invisible in plain sight, we're
grown ourselves with children of our own.
I mean, the spinning Earth whirls east
and a dog walks wagging by.
I can't explain.

Inflexible, garrulous, sad, anymore
we're our own full-time jobs.
Wasn't Dad the best?
Didn't light form in the doorways?
Didn't the mailman come?
Look Jane. Oh, turn and look.
Past the market by the playground,
here we are, so unhip, so well meaning and bizarre.

I Controlled Paul Molitor's Hitting Streak

I would never,
first of all, discount Pauly's
efforts in this thing. Naturally.
But when he homered, right off
I touched the stove slightly once
and then twice, lightly, by
the pilot. Really,
partly, it was heat and touch
that did it, you know, kept
the whole thing going. That
and certain thoughts I can't
get into here except, now, what's
the spot where the breath turns
and starts the other way?
Right there I shut my eyes, always,
every home game first and third
at bats. How that works
I won't get into either
but it wasn't all to keep his hitting
or his health and spirits up or
the team itself alive
or Wisconsin tops in dairy or the U.S.
free or even to make you think a little more
of me personally, which is, believe me,
beneath me.
Listen: I have reasons.

Blue cap, satin jacket, same
bus Wednesdays.
I love you.
Burn this.

Dear Mr. Whitman

> Vivas for those who have failed.
> WALT WHITMAN

My husband,
and don't put the blame
there, for if you had ever heard
about his life you would wonder how
he has found out enough bad luck
to call him a failure.
As in the case of the Plymouth.
A pleasant blue, decent rubber,
few dents, new door, but he
wouldn't know where
it came from first
thanks to his friends.
To make the point:
he did not apply for bad luck nor
did he atsk for it.
What do I mean?
After class last night professor
said you—
may I say Walter?—
work as a nurse so you
would surely see things as regards
to difficulties. Walter, you would go far
to find a man to go bust as much as Mike.
As for the vivas, Thanks
but never mind, Mike said.

Never mind and forget it, he said
for he has other feelings that vivas
are of little or no help.

    I tried,

    Trudy

Ray

There was something he'd done:
left the hose on or let
the dog out or
strewn his clothes around.
I didn't know.
What happened afterward
I didn't understand enough to mention
and it would have been stupid besides.
We were twelve
and Peter and I were outside
and Peter's father
opened the porch screen door
and stood there facing the yard.
Ray's face was red and he told Peter,
Come over here.
So my friend walked over
and he caught some hell, not a lot
but enough. I don't know
where my parents were
but our green Dodge was parked
by Peter's family's garage and I climbed
on the hood to see the way Ray's lecture ended.
There was, How could you, and, Why don't you,
and, Sorry, Peter said and then a pause and Ray
took a seat on the steps. Then
Peter smiled and Ray leaned just forward
and held him a moment, and gently,
like their lives depended on it.

Les Waverly: Secrets in Conversation

Dear Friends,

Why take my "easy course"? Well, why indeed.
Well, too often I would find myself "tongue-tied"
before now. Like you, I had quickly soon found out
where I was surely sinking in my aim of the future.

The point being that it was magnified in my mind
in the fact that I was *frequently not progressing*
in a particular manner.

Take my easy course, buy my simple book or tape,
for I could go all day as I am never at a loss of words
for any longer since discovering it:

>   —Popularity plus
>   —Gala functions
>   —On the phone
>   —Key phrases
>   —Punch line
>   —Light touch

In my simple book or tape, which I will pass on
cheaply with it, I give my personal regards that
you could be ugly as a foot but they would believe
anything and you are likewise aimed in the road
of life by following in the superb ways laid down:

—Dig up a sinking conversation
—Breed sincerity
—Light touch
—Ice-breakers
—Listen between the lines
—Business lunch

Therefore, if you ask me, "Les, honestly, how do you do it?" Or, "Les, how may I get ahead or be polished in a gathering?" you will either shortly be a shiny example or a complete refund.

Fast Loans

You walk in, take
a left past outboards
down the rifle aisle
and there's a woman
in heels: hotpants, pregnant,
stereo, gum.
The boyfriend's older—
twenty tops—
wears a plastic jacket
with its zipper missing.
Billy, she calls him,
Billy, I don't mind, and, Billy,
Honey, go ahead, she says.
He loves her, he says,
shoves her watch across the counter,
takes a ten. You try a smile,
try again and give up.
Outside there's the slightest
smell of exhaust and light traffic
but it's spring and it's sunny
and soon you're all three waiting
for the bus next door.
Beside the man there's a pint
bottle in a paper sack.
Beside the woman there's clothes.
In a moment the man bends
over and into her lap.
The woman looks up.
So maybe you wish him harm?

Or maybe their hard luck
looks stupid?
Is this it?
No.
The point for you is how he's paused.
The point is her hand
along his back and your own life
years out of reach.

Personal Reasons

One day you might have sat down
just this way and thought about gold.
Or maybe
it was sackcloth
or chronic misfortune.
Maybe it was foreign cathedrals.
Who knows? You might
have noted the way each night
plants breathe as much for you
as for anyone on earth.
But it might have been anything.
It might have been two spoons
tucked tight together
nightly at the rear
of a cluttered shop in southern Prague.
You might have imagined
each spoon as a half
the other's armor in a drawer
full of knives and forks
and tea balls swung by tiny chains.
Well, there's no real telling.
You might have considered
Pacific tides or hats or,
for that matter,
for strictly personal reasons,
the way some tribe changes
an arrangement of sticks at dusk
and lifts the moon

like a bright tin wafer high
over the farthest trees.
In such a way,
in your version,
inevitably as the soft news
passed through stems
your life speaks as well:
planets, liquor, envy, round vegetables,
even love.

Twenty-something

I sold my flute,
I sold my watch and my chair and my bed
and gave away my books and my TV and I took
the Greyhound bus to a town in Kentucky.
I thought I'd start over.
I thought if I could see things just as they are
(this street, this curb, sky, bottle cap, ballpoint)
I'd find out the real and the right now.
I'd locate the temperate,
gentle center of my life.
And so I walked a lot.
I'd think, Here I *am,* and, This is *it.*
I'd think, *These* trees, *this* park, *this* life.
This is *it.* This *is* it.
But what are you *doing?* my sister asked.
First she called and then she drove down from Wisconsin.
We were standing outside Kramer's Department Store.
Maybe I wasn't so sure anymore.
I guessed I didn't know.
I said, I'm living.
A city bus passed and somebody waved.
Then a dog walked by.
This, I said.
And then I said it again.

We Choose Our Parents

I'd liked one couple in La Paz,
but they were too short.
There was another outside Spokane
selling bait, but they were too loud or too
smart or something. I don't remember.
With the pair I chose I
liked the way his arms fit
behind hers at the sink.
That was part of it. I liked
that he stammered and how she
was proud when he watched stars
and made notes at his desk.
She could help him back to Earth.
But the night I chose this pair
there'd been words said.
There'd been a silence and more words
and a long pause and some shouting and I knew
how he wanted to sit down—or
they both did—and wouldn't.
There was a way she'd have her mouth
and a way he'd walk around to keep
from crying. Then, later,
they'd been quiet a while when
there was a telephone call,
and when my father hung up my mother
switched the radio on by the stove.
It could have been Armstrong or Sinatra or
Dorsey, I don't know. But

I remember how my
father asked her, softly and then
even again, if she'd possibly dance
just one and allowed as how
he himself wouldn't mind.

The Call

I wonder how he held the phone,
in his right hand or his left.
Had he let it ring and ring?
And when he'd answered
and acknowledged who he was
and said yes and yes again and said his name
and spelled it and listened while someone
told the awful news,
then did he close his eyes?
And did he tell my mother right away
or wait and live with it alone a moment?
My father never mentioned.
Whether it was a sheriff or a railroad man
or volunteer he never said.
He never spoke of it.

It was my mother though
who told how one September night
not three weeks after they were married
someone called this young man,
less than half the age I am today,
to say his parents were dead, were killed,
or they were nearly certain anyway and they
were sorry (they'd have said that) but it was for him
to come, that night, if possible,
and make a positive ID.
It was the worst train crash in Pennsylvania history.
And I think of how he must have
put the phone down, a black Bakelite receiver

with a brown cloth cord, and slowly
turned to face a wall or window.
And I wonder whether it was here
my mother walked to where he stood
and placed his hand in hers
and whether she kissed him then.
I wasn't there of course and never saw him cry.
But I wonder.
I wonder that it was not because
she kissed him he was crying but
that anyway she kissed him,
and, anyway, he wept.

Wichita 67204

Think of a certain package mailed to Kansas.
The world's saddest postman—
we'll call him Dick—
slits the package open on lunch break
weeping and swearing he'll change
his whole life starting tomorrow.
He samples half the cherry-filled bonbons,
pockets the Diamonelle ring
and the black satin panties and in all
his shame folds a twenty in the note signed,
Forever, Morry. For now,
forget the man across the street
pouring coffee and forget how his watching
the whole bleak scene prompts his
quitting work the same day
to take up ant farming and vinyl repair.
At least someone's made happy.
For now, attend to a woman who has
her whole life wanted only to marry.
Think of her hands and her pale yellow dress
and think of how, still standing at her door
and watching the postman drive away,
she flips six poked chocolates
to her neighbor's cat and burns a cherry-
smeared letter on the kitchen floor.
In a moment think
of the woman run weeping
from the house to the bus stop
and picture a last tiny spark from the letter jump

to this week's Sunday paper by the door.
But how quickly ads and comics start
to smoke! And look how Fashion glows
and waves, then moves so softly
toward that little rug! Now
picture how in fifteen minutes
half the house is filled
with fire and ruined. Never mind
that in two days the woman puts the blame
on poor Morry either.
Also, never mind
that in just three weeks she winds
up in the arms of the ant man.
No. Instead, think simply of sadness.
Think of sadness and think of disappointment
filling a tiny, flag-colored government truck

all day. Think of the postman's first
move toward the package and of how the relentless,
gentle pressure of loneliness brings another's
home to rubble. Of course,
this is your choice naturally.
But for now, for right now,
think of misunderstanding too.
And think of the rich,
full lives of others.
And consider some
chance at love in your life straight
out the window partly because you wouldn't listen
or bend when it counted, true, but mostly—
and correct me if I'm wrong in this—mostly,
because of how things happen to wind up
when it's not your fault at all hardly.

An Old Story

Once there was a weary farmer
and his nervous wife.
Picture their leaking roof and downer cows,
and consider their flooded fields and ruined corn.
There'd been his cheating
and her temper and even the boy
(not his) just six, and how
she wouldn't control him.
Now one night she was basting a goose
when three mice crossed the kitchen
and climbed over the stove.
It was odd—as far as blind mice go,
as far as any mice, you never saw such a sight
in your life, not the red-tipped canes,
not the little tin cups.
Not only that.
She said these mice love jazz music.
She said they meet every midnight under the sink.
She said the one on sax taps his pointy-toed shoes, the one
on keyboards wears wraparound shades,
and, in fancy pegged pants, the hip,
fat mouse hunkers over the drums.
And so in the farthest corner of the night,
when the moon inventories the trees and the streets
lie perfectly still, strange harmonies prevailed,
and she'd sneak through the kitchen
with her long, shiny knife.
What's true? What's ever true.
Maybe they chased her,

but the more she saw the less she'd say.
Still, she was known all over for these marvelous
breads, pies with exotic ingredients, stews with the chewy,
delectable morsels the whole town devoured
with a little pepper and a pinch of salt.

Valley Road

Once, where our street
curved by a peeling ranch house, a car
ran over a possum.
And then a crow, overeager, feasting,
inattentive, was itself struck and crushed
because there was the whole story in feathers and fur.
So my friend, slow motion pitching,
turned—there was a kind of spell—
my friend turned and said,
You're older, you'll die first.
It was a late-summer midafternoon.
What would it be not to be here?
We talked it over.
Beside the road a dog barked then lay
in a palate of sunlight under the trees.
There was a woman though, a neighbor
pulling weeds in a yard nearby.
Intent, too serious,
she looked up as we passed,
and to think of it now is to remember
my friend's splayed glove and blue-visored cap.
To think of it now is to remember feeling glad
to be the age we were.
We do our best, it's true, we persevere,
and yet, as inevitable as the thought of another,
better life comes the sudden ease with which
I'm looking back: this friend I'd had,
and the age we'd been,
and this neighbor, Mrs. Ploetz, leaning
over and looking up, and then starting to wave.

Edward Hopper, Morning Sun 1952

It isn't just the plain, pale room
she's staying in or even that her luck's run out
so much as how the sky surrounds
the roofs and seems as close
to hopeful as she's seen in years.
But there's a way the sun
now illumines her face and legs and forms
a four-foot square across the wall,
a perfect blank that makes her want
to add this up. Again,
and again, she's trying to get it straight:
this trip, and what and why she left
and where she's going anyway.
The afternoon will come and night,
and there'll be laughter in the hall
or traffic in the street, and she'll think
of how easily happiness happens,
and how it's that skilled, unemphasized
working of the will she cannot, quite,
give up on or go after.
Her arms which encircle her raised knees
provide no comfort and she'll picture
the reaching curve
that's left her in her pink slip
watching the midsized midwestern city
she will not hope to understand.
And if by learning to recover
and persist it's injury and failure

lets us live, she'll puzzle forward,
like anyone, a fury of silent trying,
and the moon, as contemptuous of effort
as the Earth, the moon will say only,
Oh, like that, just, Oh.

Chloral Hydrate 500mg May Repeat Times One as Needed for Sleeplessness

One night you wake up
with the TV humming and you
lie there. There's music
downstairs and you turn over once
more resting one arm over
your face. Of course,
why in this world anything happens
no one knows but
after a moment you think of Mozart
pulling on his brass-buckled shoes
and right away you think of Willy Shoemaker's
saddle and George Patton's belt and how
it happened each steer whose hide served
these men took its own particular
last step some May 18th
or August 3rd or other.
Possibly Mozart's rocked toward a white
picket fence which itself held three
crows perched like quarter notes.
Possibly not. As for the general's steer
and whether its hooves sunk into
some farmyard mud like tanks, well,
this is likewise shrouded in mystery.
The point here though, the real
point, is why is it anything happens
at all? Take June 23, 1963,
the night a certain four-door blue
Ford Fairlane cruised Key West.
It was ten past ten and at the wheel a man

sat chewing gum and planning a life
when suddenly, making a hard left
off a street where Frank Sinatra
himself once broke a new
lizard watch strap reaching for change,
the man dropped a hot ash on a suede
jacket mended by a woman who herself gained
fame in a liquor store heist.
He braked hard and swerved left scraping
a parked bus and delaying his life two hours
therein meeting and one day wedding
the block's fifth strongest human.
Now forget leather items.
What is it about your own third grade
teacher's limp print dress or

her late first cousin's stepbrother's
breath or burnt squash or sheer will
that some particular evening
with the couple downstairs long
gone to sleep and the moon over two
fat, black ants racing for crumbs,
a certain used flute salesman
in a seersucker suit and a blue knit cap lifts
his right thumb like a tiny
pink boot to hitchhike west and start
his life all over? Or,
say, for example, doesn't?
Won't?

1-900-CHAT

> People where you live waiting to talk to
> you now
>
> TV AD

So I hope this reaches you, I mean,
I didn't want to call at first, or, I did,
I do, it's just I'd think, If not now when?
And then,
Well, just not now.
I mean, I'd think of someone,
friendly and alone and I'd picture Johnson Street
and Orton Park, and I'd picture someone
in a yellow dress; I'd picture someone
reading, someone sewing, someone
with a cat. Another rides the bus
but has her cell phone while a dark-haired
someone steps indoors to check her messages.
Two more make drinks and others,
laughing, slender, patient, seem
content to watch TV.
Or sometimes I think of the end
of an endless long chain of events:
before now I was shoveling snow
and before that I was talking to Richard
and then zipping my jacket, then
tying my boots and then rinsing a cup,
and before that I was reading in bed,
and then it was night and then day,
then night and then day,

and last month and last year and so I go
faster and farther until there's no one
and nothing and then just God
at his big desk inventing the moment.
In fact, I think of eternity stretched in every direction
and I think of the first half back to God and up
to me again, a muddle of circumstance
and baffled will, boots pooling
water by the door, gas fire
blazing, a secret to myself.

WWII Plane Found on Moon

HEADLINE FROM *WEEKLY WORLD NEWS*

A girl stands outside a tackle shop
reading *World News*. It's mid-August.
She pulls off her jacket tugging at her
left sleeve with precisely the force used
to land the brown trout mounted
over the doorway behind her.
As for other facts linking this
girl and some thirty-five-year-old baker
who'd only caught that prize
trout because he'd quit work
and gone fishing one late afternoon,
notice how the button that pops
off the girl's jacket sits for a month
at the bus stop and winds up
in the hands of a man who thumbs the clump
of damp thread on the backside thinking
of his father in the next town
growing older beyond him. Isn't this
the father who passed to within 3/8ths of an inch
of the baker's sixth grade teacher's ex-wife
outside a grocery in Braintree, Mass.?
And wasn't this only because the father had leaned
over to pick up a backdoor key cut
by a man with a hat the color
of the shoes of the girl reading *World News*?
So isn't this the way things happen?

What's the girl say exactly?
Or what can the baker find out
in his brown chair thinking and thinking?
What about these people?
And how is it they've entered
this strange life together?
Why on Earth?

Mings Imperial Palace, October 1975

You think that is a secret, but it never has
been one. Lucky # 5, 7, 27, 41

Dick Blanco was there.
It was autumn, late Ford, early Carter.
There was high-minded Allen and Sol from Chicago.
There was Janet, and Eddy and Kim too, Kim
whose Top Fashion Economy Wig Shop
on Limestone and Main was clearly in nosedive mode.
We had a good time and Sol made a speech.
Dick Blanco spilled tea all over the place.
But you could say it was like it is now
except it wasn't now, or not yet.
You could say that needing God, and needing sex,
and culture, flattery and triumph, it was
almost the same.
I don't know.
But afterward we walked to the corner.
The trees had adorned themselves in yellow and red,
and it was dark and growing cool and what sky there was
the eye had to try for.
It must have been Allen,
I think it was Allen, who said a joke,
and we were laughing and we continued to talk
until Kim said goodnight, and then we all
said goodnight and somebody waved.
It was like it is now except it wasn't this town,
it wasn't this street, this littered kitchen, this
leaky pen, this page, this present.

I don't know.
If it wasn't a secret, if
it isn't, we wondered then too:
To be summoned out of nothing,
but for what?
Sol shivered a little, it was chilly,
and from its glassy depths life flashed
its muddled instructions and we headed home,
unlikely, and hopeful, and alone.

Free Throw

It's thirty years ago.
The sky's a sidewalk gray
and there's snow piled over the curbs.
The rule is the first to miss
hits ten more and the other goes inside
to keep count through the storm door.
Today it's you inside.
Your friend's mother sits drinking
colas and something. She's messy
and thin and when she looks up
you watch your friend's
breath make white trumpets at
the rim. He warms his hands
and shoots. A neighbor kid slips
and takes a dive on the ice.
Your friend hits three and misses
and shoots and misses and with each
shot the backboard jangles where the bolts
are loose. The mail arrives.
Your friend spins and shoots again
and misses and shoots
and when you think of it,
when you're quiet and think
of the whole scene now,
you think of the mailman's blue-
striped suit and trimmed mustache.
You think of his right arm resting
on a belt of keys. Of course,
here he's waiting with you,

beside you, for something—maybe
ten elegant, effortless hooks from your friend
or even your own miraculous set shot
straight over a mile-long cloud and a passing plane
then straight down and bouncing
off two chimneys and a telephone pole,
through that cheesy Sears hoop and
into your own outstretched right hand as gently
as that. Maybe your friend's
mother's watching with you. Or maybe
the kid next door jumps up off the ice
or the sun comes out
or there's a bird someplace.
You begin again.
There isn't a sound.

House of Chong

Frank, pay the goddam bill,
she said, drunk and easily
over eighty. Then she sat down
again, hard. She'd been
to the Ladies for the third time
at least, not that all this affected me
exactly or that those beat
white mismatched shoes and three
coats and elegant hat and tool kit
changed anything either.
It wasn't that. Also,
it wasn't the way her male friend
stood there just clearly wild about her
or the way the Chinese cook stood
smiling himself despite two
returned fried rices and a spilled
scotch and all that shouting. He
knew something, yes,
but that night I paid up and stepped
outside and there were city noises
far off and the lightest breeze ever.
I mean, I left so oddly sad
and happy both that night. Really,
it was more that I'd looked up.
It was more that I'd stopped
eating and reading and just looked up.

Kodachrome

The too white sky,
overexposed, in real life had to be blue,
especially then.
You're on the bench in the yard.
You're wearing a sleeveless white blouse
and long skirt.
You're relaxed, legs crossed.
Your right arm rests over your lap,
not formal a bit, but just so.
I took three shots of you standing—
by the hedge, by the hedge, and by a tree
(one shows a corner of the house next door)—
and you're smiling in each,
or we were, I know we were.
It's amazing to think of it, amazing
to remember how hopeful
we were, and we were hopeful, at ease
and in step, but hopeful—that's the thing—
and, yes, I'll say it: happy.

Road Kill

The first man can't
get work. Okay,
and it's been a while. For his buddy,
the one with the terrible teeth, who's had,
shall we say, an employment problem himself,
there's a matter of a bad check. But
they're driving up county M one
late Saturday afternoon
and they're talking: first it's the check
and then work, and then it's the driver's side
window and the tires and, finally, it's all these animals—
squirrels, birds, skunk, and a possum and
a small dog—all struck and bounced
into the breakdown lane or split open
and squashed. And once,
at the crest of a small hill, there's a gray
squirrel mashed flat as a rug with his tail
stuck straight up. So the man
with the bad teeth just
touches the brakes and turns to his friend
and starts in with this smile. Defiant, he says,
and keeps right on smiling—
Almost defiant!

—For Andy Kraushaar

Bat Boy Escapes

HEADLINE FROM *WEEKLY WORLD NEWS*

She called our home *unfrequented*—
is all I know my mama
kept the curtains closed.
She rinsed my wings,
she clipped my claws,
she lay of a summer's night supine across
her tile-style, blue-fleck
Domco linoleum.
Is all I know she slipped and hit
her pretty noggin on the kitchen counter.
I said, Goodbye.
I said, God bless,
and stepped outside.
It was strange, the opened sky so far away,
the moon-saddened lawns,
and somewhere
someone's radio played so softly
I could hear a girl beside it hum along—
Hello, I whispered.
And again, Hello.
O here between the car wash and the fabric store,
here in our town park with three swings,
I feast on whining flies.
I sleep in the trees.
O here in the wide world, wild, free
and thirty-five, I thank my lucky stars.

Falling Brick Kills Local Man

It's simple: it happened
so was always going to happen.
Always he'd paddle eight
silent hours in sleep, and always morning would come.
He'd choose his brown suit and change his mind
and choose his blue pants, yellow shirt, fancy
socks, and black shoes.
Always he'd leave at 8:21.
And always he'd walk down Vaughn Street,
and there'd be a siren, a dog's bark,
boots thrown over a phone line—
if there were signs they were too few to read.
Still, always, if it was habit and hard work
that brought him this far, if it was
laziness and luck, what would happen
would happen because moonlight illumined
the forest floor, it would happen because he never
ran backward, because the Earth spins east,
wood floats, metal rusts.
It would happen because.
It would happen because a little dust by the curb
formed the shape of a thumb, and if it was overcast or bright,
if dark clouds trailed a slow train steaming east,
if spectacular white clouds crossed
a stand of snow-graced pines, always
everything was lining up and merging
and making way, and there was nothing not involved,
and his life, that bright puzzlement under which

the pavement moved, always his life
would be ending at ten.
First, a blue truck would round the corner, cough,
and stall uniquely by the bank.
There'd be a smidgen of music.
There'd be somebody reading, somebody
running, somebody smiling, and, as not
yet arrived in right now,
a little cellophane waving in a bush.
And the socks—did I say?—
silk with white stripes: just right.

Jack

When I said don't run he ran faster.
When I said quit now and he could see up my
dress he slowed down, fine,
though as far as the view went: no way.
My name is Jill. I'm forty-five
and there's things you remember.
I remember we started to climb
so I said Jack, Jack leave off with the shoving.
I remember I told a story, counted backward, said
a secret and what happened happened, anyway, period,
because it did, and he could have died they said,
lost an eye. But it's nice out,
early autumn, and I'm hanging the wash when
suddenly from up the street rolls by this
hat on its brim like a hoop,
so I picture myself as seen by myself
watching this hat as if there could be nothing
in the world so sensible and real and I think of Jack.
He's dead ten years of course, but yet in the plain
clarity of his absence it seems miraculous,
all of it.
So long story short. He tripped and pitched
forward and he couldn't grab my arm because
he wouldn't let the bucket go—there's no lesson there,
not for him—god or no god it's blind chance that
lets us live, but there came this silence
and a breeze went by.
And as I got to my feet
I could see my uncle's cottage and I could see the fields

and the lake and I made this picture of all of it,
myself in my white dress making
this picture of myself in my
white dress regarding the fields
and the lake and my friend, too, one arm
over his head, opposite leg drawn up as though
swimming in place.
He could have died and so forth,
you know, but I knew he was fine,
twelve years old, you know these things—
but there came this silence, as I say, and I thought,
Here I am and I'm twelve
and I'm standing here.
And I was, too, I was standing there,
and I remember the sky was a white bowl,
and I remember through the leaves I could see
our cottage and the winding road, and how the bucket
lay beside him and sunlight wobbled the puddle it made.

Schuster

> According to (official) records Mr. Schuster
> has never served in the Marine Corps.
> Another red flag came when Schuster
> failed to properly arrange the 20 or so
> military ribbons on his uniform when he
> served as a bugler at veterans' funerals,
> said Vrana, a city alderman.
> ASSOCIATED PRESS

A breeze came, leaves fell.
Seven soldiers fired three rounds each,
and I'd played so beautifully that when I turned
I saw the sister weeping.
I know it's crazy, as a child I'd will
a little ruin just to watch: skipping school
or stealing, it wasn't just
the risk, the kick was getting caught,
the wash of shame so rich it hurt my teeth.

Once, I was waiting for the bus to work
and when it came I simply stood there.
The next day it happened again,
and the day after that. I wanted to work,
it's just, it's strange: I think of how my wife
walked out or what it was
to stand there while she packed, I mean
I could have made it right or tried except that
nothing *reached* me like disaster.

It was a day gig, the sky an endless, autumn blue,
and even as I played, especially then, and later
as we crossed the lawn, there came
a moment where I knew they knew,
a sergeant first, then someone else,
and then the family, and it felt so weird
I stood there in their midst and grinned,
as dumb as dirt—and this, I can't explain, this
too was beautiful.

Unencumbered

> ... because when it's pool day we ask
> people to put in like five bucks, so if you
> wasn't there or you didn't put five bucks
> in, sorry.
>
> <small>One of eight ConAgra meat packers after learning of their $365 million Powerball lottery win</small>

I couldn't make my mind up.
Sure, I said, and then, No thanks I guess,
and then I took my wallet out, and so he waited—
I give him that, he waited—but
I had a car note due plus rent so never mind.
It was a night shift and when our break time came
I bought a Coke and watched him smooth and fold

eight fives, and wink, thumbs up, and truck
across the street to purchase tickets.
It was Monday when they won and I
was working forklift, and they were all
about their plans and parties so I sat there,
stupid as a sack of ham and thought of happiness,
and I thought of my father too,

I thought of how the whole notion
alit on his brow after work.
You know, I could see it too, I could tell,
because he'd be reading the mail
when he'd disappear a little bit.
My mother sat in the yellow sling chair
and my father on the couch with foam

bolsters upholstered in denim.
They'd talk some then,
read a little, smoke and drink,
and there'd be a freighted,
old world sigh, and ice clinking,
and they'd walk to the kitchen for seconds.
She'd mention So-and-So's poor planning

or Whooz-it's divorce, and there'd come this
shushing conversation by the stove,
and he'd stand at the window
winding his watch.
What did he see?
It was another life, easier, maybe,
but better was the point, and I thought of glory

and love, but I thought of a tall white
house on a high hill overlooking a lake.
I thought of a wide-gated, tree-lined drive
into which a smiling couple turned in a yellow
convertible, the woman waving once in greeting
and goodbye, but unencumbered
was the point, and lucky too.

The Message

> I will send your message into outer space
> by means of radio waves for just ten dollars.
>   <small>Advertisement received over the internet</small>

I saw, shot into the starry shoals, wavelets
of adverbs, fat adjectives, and earthly nouns.
For wasn't this my own half page—
and only a sawbuck!—
aimed past Pleides to Heaven?
Look: God shuffling down His Holy Hallway,
reading His mail, lending an ear, now weeping, now
cruel, companionable, whispering, nearly
visible, nearly merely a mortal
and combing his striking
white million-mile beard, all the sweet while
razing Chicago, filling the prayer lines, making
a girl trip twice and misspeak as though
of her own undoing.
For hadn't I, too, shit-canned a right marriage,
bollixed a decade? Hadn't I
stood half my life long on our torn
planet's moonstruck lawn and worried my
sorry heart half to pieces?
Hadn't I, didn't I, deserve an audience?
On that clear night
I stood beneath the wish-worn stars,
the soft-talking maple, the thinnest
scarves of stray thought passing around me,
and I began to pray:
Hello, you don't know me but . . .

Tonight

Whatever it is about this poor schmuck
crashing his beater Plymouth into a light pole
then scaling a chain-link fence in socks and no shirt,
cheek bleeding, Mets cap backward,
I'm not sure but suddenly
he's running through somebody's yard
and half vaulting, half falling over a trashcan,
he trips into the street
where he's hit by a bus.

He scrambles up and five cops cuff him
and yank him and drag him to the flashing
black and white where they take care—careful—
he doesn't bump his head getting in.
So on this mid-autumn Saturday night
it seems to be God's way
to let this sad man stick up an all-night store
and show the whole bleak story
on the TV in front of which,

in order not to think about Louise,
I imagine those strange cells that move along
the bloodstream looking to colonize and multiply.
And I can see the planning and packing too,
and I picture them waving to friends and setting sail.
Adenoma, she's told me.
And I'd bet she was no more than leaning over
to pick up a key when the first cell got restless,
tying her scarf or rinsing a pear or

buying a brush when the first cell ship
steamed slowly north to a spot in her lung.
If there's something to learn here I don't know
but I think of the rich cells chatting with
the handsome captain and I imagine the poor cells
slurping soup in steerage, but even now
as the young man with the scraggly beard
and torn pants grins into the camera
I imagine it must be God's way

to arrange that I lie on the green couch with white trim,
God's way to arrange a magazine opened to page
eighteen, a dime by the door, a pen on the chair,
the neighbor's dog's now continual barking
through which I hear the last of the traffic:
a car and now another car,
a couple of semis double clutching, one
with a cargo of ballpoints maybe, a second
with a trailer of wing nuts and canvas shoes.

Prognostic

There'd been
a kind of accident, by which he meant
he'd somewhat shoved
his mother's cat inside the freezer.
Before school, he said, to cool it down
because it scratched him.
Then he'd forgotten.
And then he'd remembered
so I biked on over.
There was a moment though,
the one before the one I'd tell him what
I knew he knew, when we were standing there.
The kitchen door was open and we heard the neighbor's
kid skate up the sidewalk.
But there was Bob regarding me regarding the cat,
and there was this moment like a room
except invisible and still,
and I thought of a high, blue, cloud-strewn sky
the way I'd seen it from a plane,
lion face, monster dog, and running muscle man,
and suddenly I'd glimpsed the Earth again,
wonderful, ridiculous, and sad.
Bob propped the cat against the toaster,
feet ceiling-ward, and then the phone rang.
It was fall I think,
eighth grade if I remember,
and I said, He's dead.

This Is What Happened

It must have started the moment I left,
on the way down the steps, if there were steps,
to the car, if there was one, and it must have continued
all that night, my forgetting,
unstoppable into the following day, unrelenting
through that year and the year after that
and the year after that—
whose place it was, why I was there.
Or just why not say it took place in discreet,
small, sensible clumps, in twos or threes, for instance:
an olive plus a scruffy fern, then the man
with the comb-over saying he's sorry.
In the following second gone forever are a set of blue
dice with a 5/8ths socket and a broken high heel.
And it wouldn't be so different
with the girl herself—first her name,
and something she said, then whatever she sat on,
and later the same day I'm peeling an orange
when her hair and her smile disappear with the sullen
blond friend to her right.
It's something like that.
In a blink, a beefy lady with an estimating look,
a purple sombrero, a little guitar.
In fact, look:
everything remaining of the whole
night disappears right down to the girl or
the shape of a girl or the idea of a girl but a girl,
anyway, talking softly in the bedroom, drunk maybe,
weeping a little.

I think it was clear outside.
But I picture dancing and laughter,
and think of a neighbor downstairs pounding
the ceiling with a broom. Or who can say the whole
night didn't amount to anything more than four
friends playing the radio
some Thursday after work, and the girl,
the sister of the landlord, not weeping so much
as simply humming, and not even humming so much
as slowly packing her bags.
I can't say except here she is in this bedroom
illumined no more by the sun or the moon
or a handful of stars than by the simple
lack of what surrounds her anymore.
The mind, singing or still, I mean,
the mind is its own place.

Mantra

One word, one word,
one word. You breathe
again and over again.
In the blue-strewn, star-pricked black,
and even from a promise
that they won't begin,
begin the delicate narratives.
Again and over again there's
your goodness and another's pride,
the near solution and half a joke,
unspoolings of passion, patience,
anger, and angst. Oh, but
nothing can disturb you now.
And so it goes. One word,
one word, one word. And not
the vulgar limerick or the note
you take because you like it, not
a breeze as gentle
as the air displaced
by almost blinking, not
the caffeine from last week
and not the debts and blessings
of a wife as sweet
as all the tea steeped,
drunk, and spilled
in China since the first lit stick.

One word.
In the grainy dark for months,
minutes like months,
over your own odd, splendid tundra,
patient as an ox,
you breathe;
you pull.

THE FELIX POLLAK PRIZE IN POETRY
Ronald Wallace, General Editor

Now We're Getting Somewhere • David Clewell
Henry Taylor, Judge, 1994

The Legend of Light • Bob Hicok
Carolyn Kizer, Judge, 1995

Fragments in Us: Recent and Earlier Poems • Dennis Trudell
Philip Levine, Judge, 1996

Don't Explain • Betsy Sholl
Rita Dove, Judge, 1997

Mrs. Dumpty • Chana Bloch
Donald Hall, Judge, 1998

Liver • Charles Harper Webb
Robert Bly, Judge, 1999

Ejo: Poems, Rwanda, 1991–1994 • Derick Burleson
Alicia Ostriker, Judge, 2000

Borrowed Dress • Cathy Colman
Mark Doty, Judge, 2001

Ripe • Roy Jacobstein
Edward Hirsch, Judge, 2002

The Year We Studied Women • Bruce Snider
Kelly Cherry, Judge, 2003

A Sail to Great Island • Alan Feldman
Carl Dennis, Judge, 2004

Funny • Jennifer Michael Hecht
Billy Collins, Judge, 2005

Reunion • Fleda Brown
Linda Gregerson, Judge, 2007

The Royal Baker's Daughter • Barbara Goldberg
David St. John, Judge, 2008

Falling Brick Kills Local Man • Mark Kraushaar
Marilyn Nelson, Judge, 2009